Hoard

Jaime Robles

Hoard

SHEARSMAN BOOKS
2013

To LLB, with many thanks

First published in the United Kingdom
in 2013 by Shearsman Books Ltd.
50 Westons Hill Drive
Emersons Green
Bristol BS16 7DF
www.shearsman.com

ISBN 978-1-84861-282-2

Interior design and illustrations by Jaime Robles

CONTENTS

White Swan 7

Hoxne 19
(lash of the tongue) 21
These spare objects 22
Gold Body Chain for a Small Woman 24
Spice boxes 28
Oak and iron locks 29
Diátrita (opus interassile) 30
Her upper arm, festooned 32
Her upper arm, festooned 33
Translation 34
Not even bones 35
Sieve 36
Four Matching Gold Bangles 37
"Utere felix, domina Juliane" 45
"Utere felix, domina Juliane" 47
Cygni 49
Sieve 50
The Hunt 51
Trove 53

Quatrefoils 57

Red Boat 67

ACKNOWLEDGMENTS 79

White Swan

Out into the river Exe children sail in kayaks
their singular voices easy in shouts and laughter—
words zigzag into words

and gather into cloth.

It is easier for you to unravel them, speaking, as you do,
their language.

.

At the iron bridge white swans cluster, and the thin walkway
suggests a passage from here to an imagined and fatal land.

> "Why is it now
> impossible for us to meet—
> we who were bound together
> like the strands of a close woven basket
> impermeable to water"

•

Outside, the sky roils in gray:

a glint within tumuli becomes a mirror or key and, below,
hanging from the bright trees, each leaf a stray declaration

lifted by wind

until the stem breaks loose from its lean connection—
spinning down to water, sidewalks, grass.

.

It was your paleness that struck me the other evening

like a match lit—
above us the ceiling catching fire.

·

The city's fringe of lights wraps the edge of the hills, the woods night-dyed:

its vivid trees of red and yellow dropped into black.

A slurry of nouns tumbles across the page.

The window resists opening, allows only a quick wintery chill.

·

Scraps of paper, swanlike, float up
collecting color on their surfaces, the water shearing off,
shuddering.

Like Persephone I have left my mother behind.
You, with your precision, would claim that she has left me,

but her death was neither her choice nor mine.

Still, she lives on, breathless, and I am caught between two lands,
her kindness pursuing,

the immediate air darkening into night.

•

I enter the silence around me: its space grown large and doorless,
denser than fur
or feathers thick at the breast—
paths lead elsewhere.

Not all silence is retraction,
its intentionality allied with small cruelties;

the coat you knit me was incomplete—
I stand before you, head tucked beneath my one white wing.

•

And the planet veers through space, resembles an afternoon in Los Angeles,
when we fashioned marbled paper on the patio:
black, gray, red and gold tangled
on the face of the pan's water, oily and unmixable,
baffled until combed into pattern.

Our fingertips stained, disappearing into the swirl-patterned surface.

Decorative paper, good for nothing but wrapping the pages of a book.

Swans glide by, their paddling feet invisible.

•

How many iterations must be written
—the curvatures of letters tracing a lip, fingers, the porch of the eye—
turning thought and sense into glass, clear and divisive?

I had forgotten the strength of silence—its mutability.

I was busy with the details of a bracelet lost many years ago
on a street filled with people walking north and south.

•

And you?

Love, too, is distant and fatal, requiring coins for the ferryman.
A viaticum of words carefully saved—

placed on the tongue

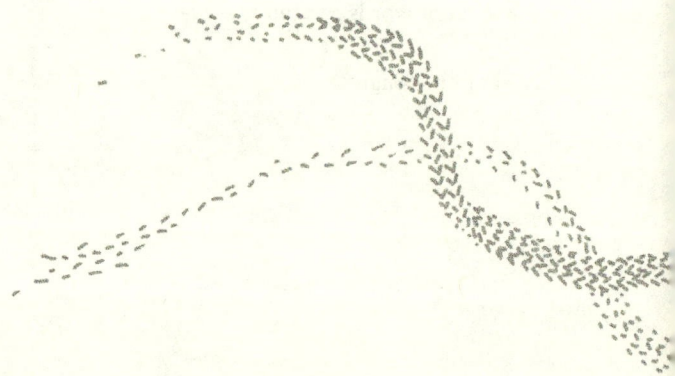

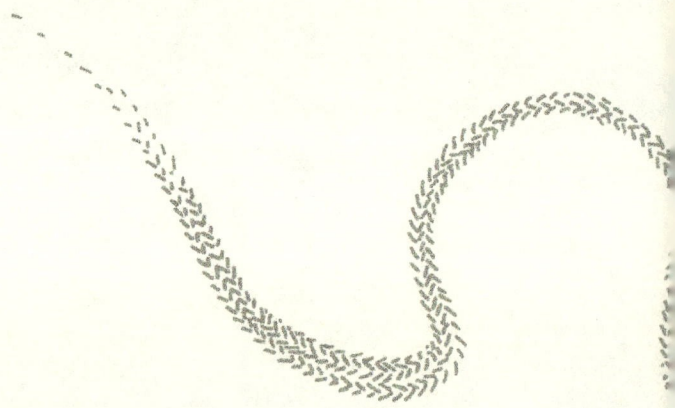

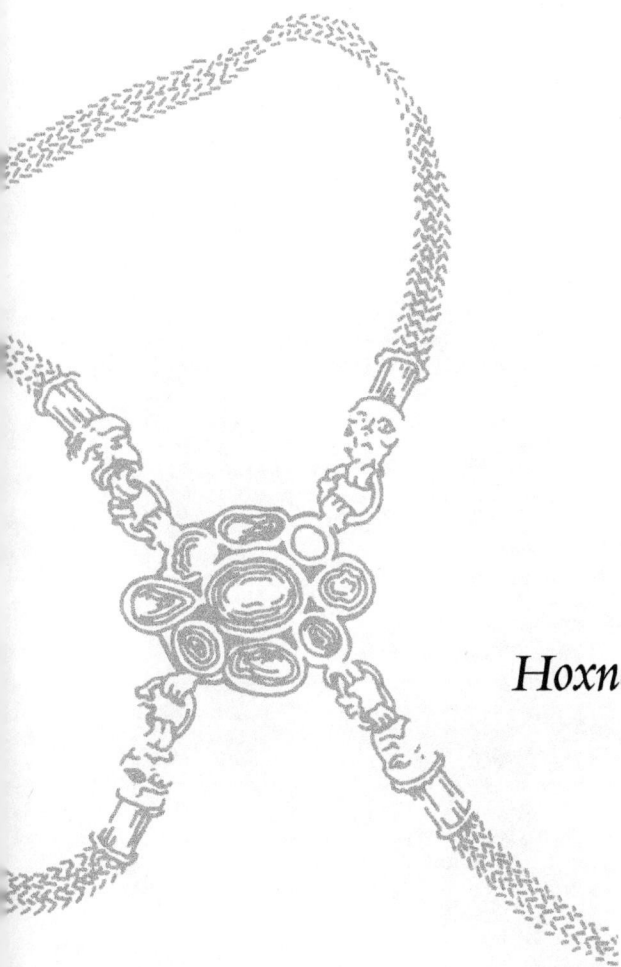

Hoxne

The findspot of the Hoxne hoard lies in the county of Suffolk, in eastern England, on the top of a spur ... between the valley of the River Dove to the west and the Gold Brook to the east."

— from "Discovery and Archeological Investigation of the Site," *The Hoxne Late Roman Treasure*

(lash of the tongue)

She steps back, carves away clumps of soil,
repaths a sentence in arachnid labor
and reveals the layered slope,
the strata of discard:

words retract into her mind, repeating,

hang back
struggle to renew
become abruptly vatic

resemble memory, or a spoon, locked beneath earth, bound into time

These spare objects

                like love

—impulsed out, slipping forward: fox paw on ice—

lie displaced from their close shelter

the worn rims
and bright faces of coins—unround
and irregular, shaved at the perimeter—

                          up from wet earth

Or, as when deterred, love revolves,
turns
in the womb—wraps inward: insistent ivy growing deep
into the ridged bark of a cedar tree.

                                            Antipodal,
and heavy, it burrows in the body's cells:

a splinter in a finger. Tangy like pepper. Floating
urgent under flesh, which folds
its thin sliver into a husk of hard winter.

Gold Body Chain for a Small Woman

"Have mercy and pity on me and let me rest my heart in you."
> —translated from French and incised in a twisted gold brooch, 14c.
> Scottish National Museum

I

Cross my heart. Drop the long X of woven chain
across the clavicle's horizontal bones: an ornament marks the junction

with stones—four-petalled stones front and back, roped:
such discs serve as calculations of the heart's orbit.

In the midst of tumult a man's voice curves—
carves lines of gold—across the body's turfs.

---

seam settling   over the seized heart
as an amulet   amethyst and garnet
resplendent pearls   passed into dust

2

Can the earth have corners? Bisected twice in perpendicular,
long loops collapsed into the retangular—.

Her breast a globe hung from the shoulder's
cross, pressing flat against the cage of the lover's

chest. A cloven circle. Stealthy in its advance, the heart passes
through gates, buries itself beneath the earth, unlooses

the foreign. Her arms flow upward—a gold cord remakes
their embrace—his arms sketch the legs of the X,

across her back, fixed. Each feels the arc of other between
them and the wide line of severance.

---

three threaded   *thick seeming and*
four fingered   *into a fulcrum each*
strand strung   *from a single terminal*

3

The bird rushes into the window. It does not see
the glass but believes its flight forward will be unimpaired, free—

pursuing the mirage of sky on the utter surface, branches of trees,
an image smeared flat, highlighted and darkened, strangely:

the flyer's reflection veers outward, hurtles head on.
Shifts in blue cloud its small eye, miniscule evidence

skims the black iris. The flyer plunges in.

4

His voice follows as precisely as a finger the chain
that paths under her arms, bright like a coin among many,

more than a thousand: edges of silver clipped, the gold
pliable, fluid. Her face, a cloth opened like a fold.

Surely something dreadful must have happened
for no one returned—the treasure left, never retrieved.

---

loop-in-loop   *links of gold*
terminals turned   *toward the center*
fused fracture   *filleted into prior*

Spice boxes

shattered

an ibex, glassy eyed,
its myriad small pieces uncovered
resoldered
in painstaking detail

a dog entwined with a rabbit

And Hercules' struggle
reduced to three inches in height:
Gaia's head
just below Antaeus' foot
his mother Earth's face

a mask, mute

Oak and Iron Locks

Once contained within the dimensions of a wooden chest
whose walls dissolved, slowly

Because the deep earth is vital as skin—
clay clinging to clay
small animals and fingers of gravity
moving beneath its liquid surface

Diátrita (opus interassíle)

—After two gold bracelets, Hoxne treasure, Roman Britain c. A.D. 400

A sheet of gold
pierced: cut
into a wall of vines

•

curling vines
or tendrils—
the air adjoining
simply that

•

a simple piercing of gold,
banded, surprisingly workable:
the metal lace-like—
its past
unseeable, shifting

•

like a voice that shifts to echo
and locates us, sprung back
from brisk walls: as if
no morsels of background
were dropped out,
mislaid, gone

•

time lies flattened,
stretched into a hoop:
pricked
into lapsed
panoramas—chinks
among cracks—crevices
openings so that

•

through the open work of tendrils
skin glistens—fine hairs
scattered and budding:
whose memory is reflexive
sited on the other side
of a punctured strip
sprouting vegetal strands
fiery vines, gold and coiling

Her upper arm, festooned

— Gold armlet, pierced and decorated. Borders are hollow cylinders.
  Between borders are eight panels ornamented in opus interrasile in four
  designs, each repeated twice.

Under his gaze her upper arm, which seems only bone,
barely fleshed,
is a pier stretching out into sea water and pleasure,
knobs at each end, planed and birdlike, seeking ligature
and the hollow sound of his footsteps—
above the smell of sky, the capacious exile of snow

An arm wrapped. The tip of his middle finger touches his thumb,
completes a current:

index finger a tube of gold, imperfectly round, scored
and imbricated with diamond shapes, scaly—battered—

and below: the smallest finger, nail pink and fresh as a sea shell

Vines, like kelp, sway in the palm of his hand, wending
toward possession and domestic habit. The never-ending
pull of tides, a drizzle of desire—oak and ivy, gold and gold

Her upper arm, festooned

glints of small birds,

eyes

the rose leaf of tongue

Translation

Within the archive of letters that flowed
from his fingers across the keyboard
she reads hindrance, recalling the not yet unfolded musk
of moth-white flowers in the powdery air of dusk

There isn't anything there, on second look,
only kerned curves and vertical strokes—
black on white—not, as she thought (the backlit
screen a veil, the image revenant),
a loss of focus behind the eyes' lens,
decking the surrounding skin with lines

Not even bones

only

silver bowls or gold

creases

whisper

confessions

singular,

inaudible

Sieve

Incised in gilt settled in the bowl
                gathering into dapples on
                a sheen of silver,

a bearded Oceanus, or the limbs of a marine creature, its shadows
waiting excavation—

a spoon meant to celebrate gods
and the body, full and

Four Matching Gold Bangles

I

Clay clasping the wrist, thumb and finger: manacled, mute.
The tongue a basket—forest of gold corrugate: scuddering
cries, muffled, fallen reeds: plaid of stalks. Speech stopped
at the first gate; in the background, disaster: a procession of doors,
each closed, each to be opened. Pushed rustling into the earth,
wrapped, the horizon a whirlpool. The soft shush of breath and heart's
outward flight quelled, fallen earthward turning—slowly,
sound withdrawn. Indwelling the coat of flesh the muscle of tongue

---

      clasping   wrist, thumb and finger:

                           the *circumference* of forest.

leaves mute

          —gold: *chuddering*

                   Speech contracts

             rustling

corrugate

speech

nets the soft breath

wresting

flesh

2

Fixing a bond, crushing the hand: slipped over. Thoughts—
urges—packed in fabric: press of soft mouth against careful mouth,
short cropped grass stifled, branch dappled. Prized bits and pieces
nested into each other; in the foreground, sentences: encircling gold
lacing matter and sound, layered like onions, rattling up from the earth;
wrapped, the perimeter of the wrist. Clink. Click. Clatter. The past's
forward flight looking back, always, turning often and again—reluctantly,
folded, replaced, altered. Indwelling the rod of bone the shatter of tooth

---

a hand slips

across

his soft mouth

lacing reluctant matter and sound

—circle of

bits and pieces

clatter

—

3

Gold flickering the wrist, vein and artery: bordered, buoyant.
Hinge of hand, jaw—molten crisscross congealed: vowel-sailing,
a tattered venetian blind: unloosed. She summons, unlocking
the gate, herding the heart: impatient, restless. Every escape
lost in the river's rising lineaments: tree, fading mist. Warbler
rushing across earth, departure a whirlpool. Lips amend the nostril's breath,
and the outward thrust of words turns earward—hissing,
sizzling touch and trill. Indwelling the disk of nail the blink of eye

---

adrift

a whirlpool

earward—

trill
of eye

buoyant

whirl

warbling eye

4

Seeding the future, a click: metallic wheels turning fingers that point.
Numbers tumble within a glass bowl, the glow of concave air sweet and
acrid. Smoke, scented of pine, fur. Inevitably, limbs nest into each other,
gold and silver. In the middle ground, silence: far under the body where
the entrance to the underworld opens up, planets encircle the sun: a wrist,
the perimeters of spoons. The bird sunk down in flight, or caged,
a signal, interstices of a pomegranate; click of the lover's teeth. Red
gushes forth, lubricates past into future—an eternal rim spinning convex walls.

---

wheels   spoons

                                        flickering

                        clatter

click

"Utere felix, domina Juliane"

—Inscription on a gold bracelet, Hoxne treasure, c. A.D. 400

A hand thrust through the circle
of space drawn by a hoop of yellow,
telling of blood and bone
in the center of nothingness

•

The bracelet in turn wraps to the wrist,
garlands her skin
with leaves, doorways

•

Her bracelet slips up and drops
as her arm rises and falls.
A hand's width holds it to the wrist.
Glimmer anchors it in the eye of an onlooker.

•

Who is to say words are without attraction:
WEAR THIS WITH JOY, LADY JULIANA

•

Gold circles endlessly,
and part of the world drops out again:

the penetration of cold
empty sky
gleam of the stream's thin casing over stone's surface
the thick paste of silt
all furrowing round paths

"Utere felix, domina Juliane"

—Inscription on a gold bracelet

Because he sees her as beautiful
he is pulled to the side
not joined but trapped in her gravity,
unbuttoning momentum

•

Though beauty unconsidered
seems like light or distance
in relief: a flight

•

The sway would fall
magnetically inscribing a caress
across her thigh—inward spills,
an unhealed bifurcation

•

There is no symmetry here even though
bracelets encircle both wrists

•

Smooth surfaces form an ecosystem:
Her mouth like the forest floor humid

indivisible, yes, teeming
Tongue's movement more than muscular—
requiring a parade of vowels;
she pulls back the hair from her forehead
revealing a frame of white froth

Cygni

And spoons tapering into birds' heads, crest,
or a sea creature, fin curving back,
black nostril and oval eye,
the concave belly a body, slick and unfeathered:

> his name (golden or perhaps sunlit)
> punched into silver, floating
>
> and cut loose from memory—
>
> A U R E L I U S
>
> —flight follows from fingertips to mouth

Sieve

The bowl of a silver spoon is a mirror
this figure is you, staring back at yourself:
a bird, or dolphin, or griffin, that moves through
and across what the planet offers: air ... water ... fire ... earth.

And because there are two of you,
time shutters open, just as now removes itself to then,

shedding on its way details—

patterns of light, and story-telling, absurd and restless.

Soup becomes clotted dirt and the color of flesh
glows thin and metallic, shakes
to a blur, like day following day, night rounding

The Hunt

Decorated with frieze of running animals, arranged in pairs, two facing left and
two confronted. Stylized trees between them; hunting. Perforated patterns form a
background.

> —Museum description of a repoussé bracelet

Round and round
limited by the yellow coils
of sky and earth
and unidentifiable plants

•

Size is variable here:
the long-eared rabbit as large as a tree or an ox
or the lion chasing

Their features hammered
out of soft flatness,
shaped by upheaval
their details woolly, or better, mime erasure

•

like love, a construct conjured from the body's
hungers, or spun off
from the wholeness of the planet,

the mammal's jigsaw
fitness.

•

A nereid
wearing necklace and bracelets, naked,
her bare feet small and crossed,
floats along
cleaved from tendrils of arteries, fibrous muscle.

She hangs on the reins of a sea creature

•

There are fewer animals than believed,
each sprung from small and intricate beats, or measures of time:
footsteps and tracks, the collapse of wood under flames,
the turquoise collisions of mountain streams,
the passage of thread and needle binding the wide
grin of cut flesh to flesh, smoke of stars.

•

He said he would call at noon and here it is:
night.

Trove

Though carefully packed they were nothing more
than extraneous. The precious stones prised
from the rings and gone

"There is no misfortune in the world equal to separation"

distance measuring absence

... counting ...

Decoration consists of alternating circles and lozenges with pierced work in centre and spandrels between. Circles have engraved star pattern, and centres of circles have pierced rosettes. Lozenges contain stylized foliate pattern and central quatrefoil.

—Description of an Anglo-Saxon bracelet,
British Museum, online catalog, 2010

Quatrefoils

First quatrefoil

four

stem to stem

radiant

Quatrefoil recursive 1

their eyelids, thin and veined, fringed
at the edge, lashes knit, lying like wet leaves across two sets
of eyes (his blue, hers brown), where the real action happens:
Each lid a half, almond shaped, like a valentine split in two

stem to stem

radiant

•

four

fingers rooted into the pad of the hand, thumb wandering
                                                    outward

rooted

.

four

stem to stem

a small umbrella broken : its ribs cracked, bent,

turning cool elegances of axes (x, y, z) into the wing
of a sea bird discarded at tide line

wave-turned over and over

                              curious

dogs and children, led by the nose, worry its angles

higher on the beach
a faded umbrella stammers structure
indomitable wood and the steel ring at the center,
          fabric unfurling from the upright pole,

                    the figures beneath leaning toward

Quatrefoil recursive 2

Children search through green grass
its wiry weave tenting pockets close to the ground
where pallid stalks hide small thoroughfares bypassing
the rare, the sought-after, the unfound

stem to stem

daystruck

•

one ... two ... three ...

two pairs of couples facing into a circle
right hands lifted, touching, forming a bridge or gate
their feet figure the wood floor with
zeros, finished and half-finished—a turn
less abrupt than expected—and eights
                                        looping

they approach touch (flickering familiar, unfamiliar)
like the first days of May

or a glass of water before thirst,
the thin transparency an intervention

its recollection in one piece

radiant

•

four

stem to stem

arms of stars spun out, caught on film light years after

Variation

In the middle of a darkened room, a light on the nightstand
forms a sphere soft at the edges,
and I pass through the chambers of my heart
following its blood's flow.

The first is white and allows no privacy.
Walls smooth as the interior of an egg.

The second and third are blue and mirrors
of each other: the air is alpine.

The fourth is dark and sticky: poplar leaves line
its muscular floor, yellow and resolute, the tissue

fallen away, leaving deft skeletons, bright flags

Quatrefoil recursive 3

1 ... 2 ... 3 ...

The rock at the heart of the clock cleaved
into two perfectly matched halves, carved out.
Two crystal discs with sawtooth edges, to which
the clock's hands are attached, placed
in the hollows, making them seem to float
and spin around the dial of their own accord ...

radiate

•

4 ...
stem to stem
around

•

4 ...

stem to stem
radiant

Final quatrefoil

heart

body

eye

Red Boat

You require me to read and reading
to step into space as if I were haltered to the sun,

assume molecules of air beneath my feet;

to walk on water, only less so

.

Clouds mass and flow,
the gaps between them opening faster than the words you speak

My history is folded into a square of page and colored with childhood ink—
its black faded to brown, a seepage away from shadow
and into time's contours—

•

The page—a packet—turns, escapes applied color,
and what lies beneath my fingertips reduces to fewer words,
insupportable and misplaced.

From what book has this page come?

I reach out for words,
their path promised me.

.

Steppingstones or mosaic tile,
the sheets realign, re-collect into patchwork.

                                        And wind-tossed,
a red boat rocks past, gone rusty from airy breaths
and the painter's imaginary hand.

•

We are reshuffled,
slip like grass

across the cheek of the face

> "Like the random pattern
> of the robe dyed with young purple
> from Kasuga plain—
>
> even thus, the wild disorder
> of my yearning heart"

Letters curve like fingers and harden into a carapace:

a question forms on the white field,
hesitations advance to black.

.

I believe you have sworn on a book with a brightly colored title page, made a pact between you and your gods.

Your mouth a red boat.

.

Forces mold each volume—two figures wrapped in black
weave into conductivity.

Out over the rooftops of London, lightning strikes.

You who met me half way,
there's no telling how words will be read:
they form a plasma

.

Or a red boat strung on copper curved
across canvas.
                    Only over pages will they peel away
and the figures disrobe into utterance.

•

The silence between syllables hangs like a question mark

and, so, touch between us melts into a brief deferral of motion.

•

Fugitive.

Our bones are hollow and the color of a quill
ink filled,
carved for flight:

birds rise from the water's surface,
a gleam of silver spilling down the feathered wing.

ACKNOWLEDGEMENTS

Many of the poems in this collection were inspired by the Hoxne
treasure, which is housed in the British Museum. The Hoxne
treasure is a hoard of gold and silver domestic items—jewellery,
plates, spoons, spice boxes and coins—a cache likely assembled by
women. In the chaos of the late Roman and Anglo-Saxon periods in
Britain, valuables were buried as a means of keeping them safe.

I would like to thank the editors of the following magazines,
where versions of these poems appeared: *New American Writing,
Shadowtrain, Shearsman, Stride, The View from Here,* and *Volt!*

My thanks to Jo Gill and Andy Brown of the University of Exeter.
Special thanks and affection to Susanne Dyckman, Hazel White,
and John Hall for their careful and insightful readings of this book
in manuscript; their thoughts and kindness shaped this book.
Thanks also to Claudia Smelser for her splendid cover design,
and to my publisher Tony Frazer, who to my amazement seems to
find my writing suitable enough. And my deep gratitude to Linda
Brownrigg—without her support this book would have remained
only a hankering, unaddressed and incomplete.

Jaime Robles published *Anime, Animus, Anima* with Shearsman Books in 2010. She has produced many of her texts as artist books, including *Loup d'Oulipo* (Woodland Editions, 2002) and *Letters from Overseas* (Woodland Editions, 2010). A frequent collaborator with composers, she wrote the libretto for Ann Callaway's one-act opera *Vladimir in Butterfly Country,* which premiered in 2011.